Shapes Around Us

Daniel Nunn

www.raintreepublishers.co.uk
Visit our website to find out more information about Raintree books.

To order:
☎ Phone 0845 6044371
🖺 Fax +44 (0) 1865 312263
💻 Email myorders@raintreepublishers.co.uk

Customers from outside the UK please telephone +44 1865 312262

Raintree is an imprint of Capstone Global Library Limited, a company incorporated in England and Wales having its registered office at 7 Pilgrim Street, London, EC4V 6LB – Registered company number: 6695582

Edited by Daniel Nunn, Rebecca Rissman, and Sian Smith
Designed by Joanna Hinton-Malivoire
Picture research by Elizabeth Alexander
Illustrations by Joanna Hinton-Malivoire
Originated by Capstone Global Library Ltd.
Production by Victoria Fitzgerald
Printed and bound in China by South China Printing Company Ltd

ISBN 978 1 406 22616 4 (hardback)
15 14 13 12 11
10 9 8 7 6 5 4 3 2 1

British Library Cataloguing in Publication Data
Nunn, Daniel. Shapes around us. – (Everyday maths)
   1. Shapes–Pictorial works–Juvenile literature.
   I. Title II. Series
   516.1′5-dc22

Acknowledgements
We would like to thank the following for permission to reproduce photographs: Dreamstime.com p.13 (© Raphotography); Shutterstock pp.4 left (© Africa Studio), 4 right (© Lori Sparkia), 5 left (© erperlstrom), 5 right (© Coprid), 7 (© Dmitriy Shironosov), 8 (© Chiyacat), 8 (© Tilo G), 8 (© Carlos Caetano), 8 (© akiyoko), 8 (© Jiang Hongyan), 8 (© Kristina Postnikova), 9 (© Beneda Miroslav), 11 (© Anna Chelnokova), 12 (© Jiri Hera), 12 (© Konstantin Yolshin), 12 (© Evgeny Karandaev), 12 (© Dmitry Naumov), 12 (© Swapan), 16, 17 (© Mariia Sats), 20, 21(© karamysh).

Cover photograph of a Palheiro Traditional thatched house, Santana village, Madeira reproduced with permission of Alamy (© STOCKFOLIO®).

Every effort has been made to contact copyright holders of any material reproduced in this book. Any omissions will be rectified in subsequent printings if notice is given to the publisher.

Contents

Shapes around us

Let's look for shapes.
It's time to play!

How many shapes can
you find today?

Circles

This is a circle.
Circles are round.

Look at this photo.
How many have you found?

Circles, circles, everywhere!

Is this window a circle?

No, it's a square!

Squares

1

4

2

3

Squares have four sides, all the same size!

How many squares are there here?

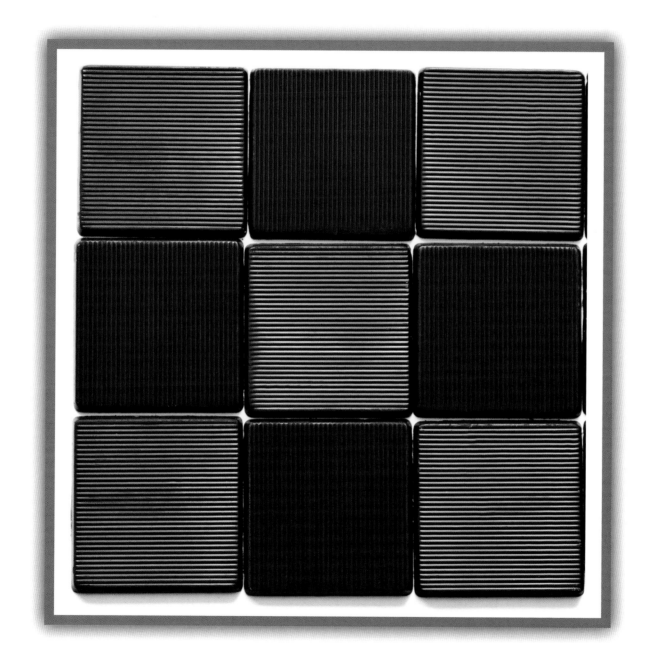

Look with your eyes!

Here are some more squares,
both big squares and small.

12

Are there squares on this cake?
Try and count them all.

Rectangles

long side

short side

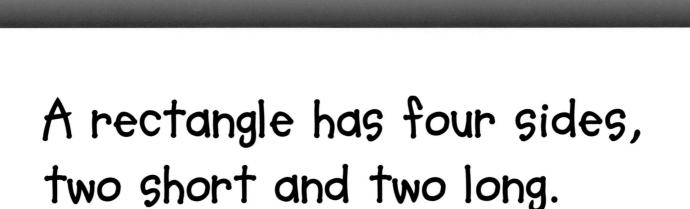

A rectangle has four sides,
two short and two long.

14

NOT A RECTANGLE

If you think it's got six sides,
I'm afraid you'd be wrong!

15

Can you see any rectangles by this front door?

I can see at least three, can you see any more?

Triangles

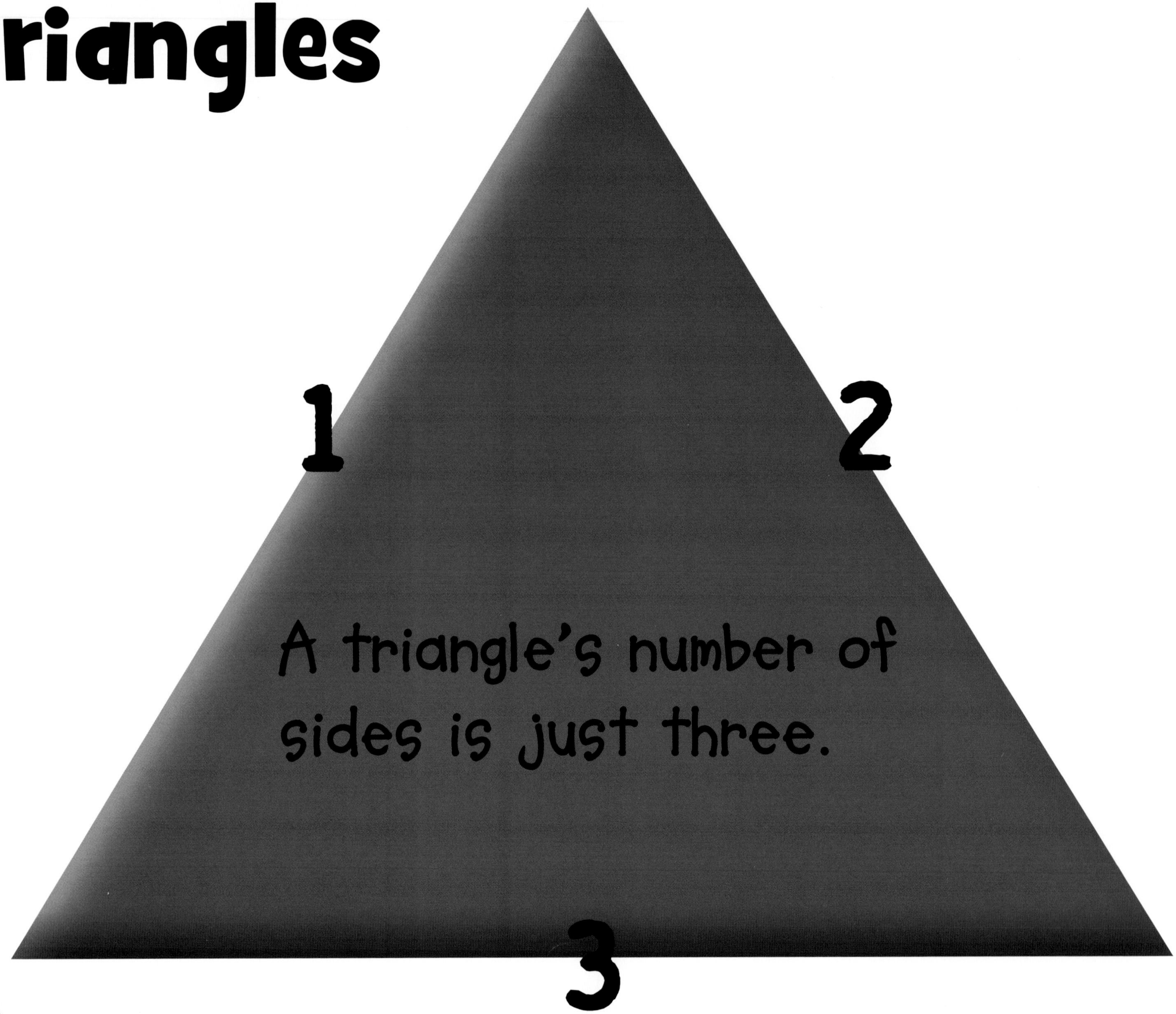

1

2

A triangle's number of sides is just three.

3

18

How many points does it have?
Can you see?

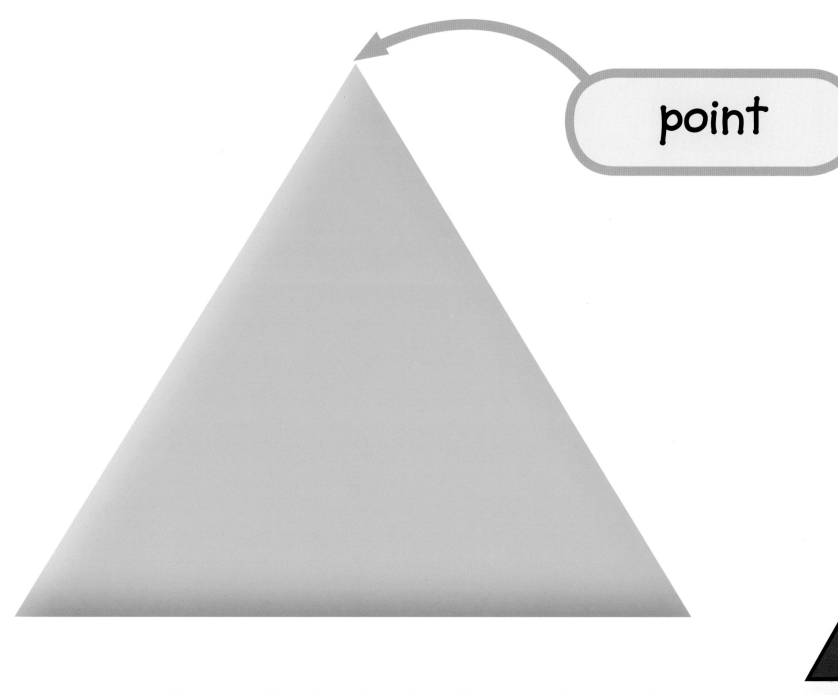

point

19

Look at this picture.
Are there triangles here?

If you found at least three,
then I'll give you a cheer!

21

Other shapes

Are there other shapes, too?
Yes, of course there are!

Do you know the names
of these shapes?

3

4

If you do, you're a star...

(And a star is a shape too!)

Answers on page 24

Index

Answer to question on page 22

Shape 1 is a hexagon.

Shape 2 is a star.

Shape 3 is a diamond.

Shape 4 is an oval.